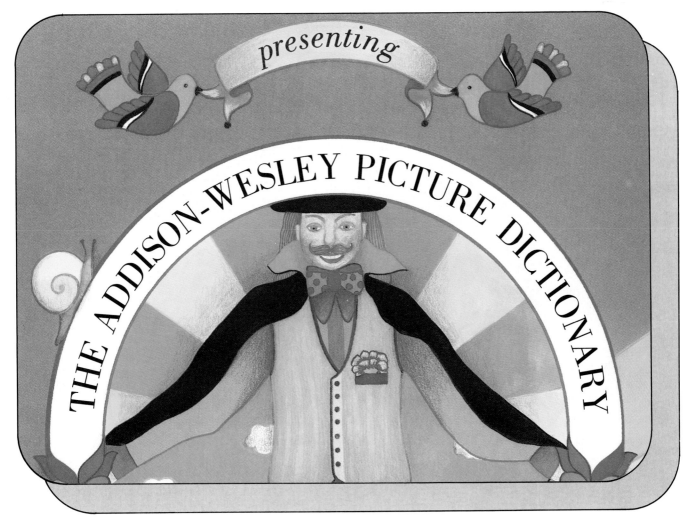

presenting

THE ADDISON-WESLEY PICTURE DICTIONARY

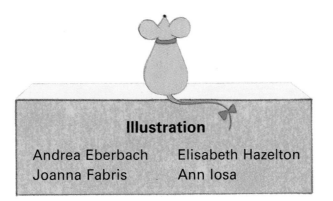

Illustration

Andrea Eberbach	Elisabeth Hazelton
Joanna Fabris	Ann Iosa

▲▼ Addison-Wesley Publishing Company

Reading, Massachusetts • Menlo Park, California • Don Mills, Ontario • Amsterdam • London • Manila • Singapore • Sydney • Tokyo

Consultants

Keiko Abe
Alma Flor Ada
Anna Uhl Chamot
Esther J. Eisenhower
Curtis W. Hayes
Ritsuko Nakata

Editorial

Judith Bittinger   Ann Strunk

Production

James W. Gibbons

Design and Art Direction

Joanna Fabris

A publication of the World Language Division

Preface

The Addison-Wesley Picture Dictionary is a unique adventure in English language learning for young children. It has been especially designed for children who do not speak English as a native language. It can also be used to enrich native speakers' first experiences in reading, since the 550 featured words have been carefully chosen from first *and* second-language high frequency lists.

The words are shown through pictures and print in two unique ways. Some words are grouped by beginning alphabet letters. Other words are grouped in meaningful context rising from a scene—an airport, a birthday party, a magic show, and so on. Each of the "letter" pages prominently features a part of the scene that the child will discover upon turning the page.

The "letter" pages provide varied practice in listening, speaking, and word recognition skills. They also offer opportunities for classifying, sorting, spelling, alphabetizing, and sentence-building activities.

The "scene" pages also provide varied practice in listening, speaking, and word recognition skills. Moreover, these pages act as springboards for discussion and use of descriptive language, for role play, storytelling, and vocabulary expansion. A continuing story line can be created for the adventurous little mouse that appears throughout the book.

Teachers and parents alike can use this delightful dictionary to give young learners an entertaining and solid start in English language learning.

See pages 64–66 for specific suggestions for using this outstanding teaching tool in classroom situations.

CONTENTS

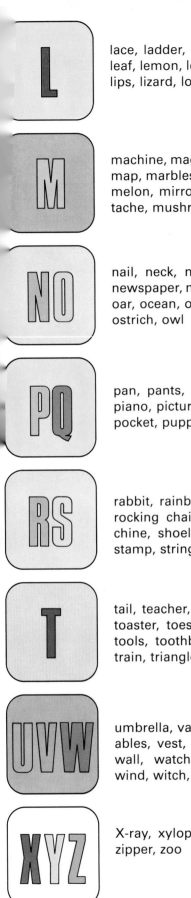

L

lace, ladder, lake, lamb, lamp, lap, laundry, leaf, lemon, letter, light bulb, lightning, lime, lips, lizard, lobster, lock, log

32–35 **Laundry,** bathrobe, belt, blouse, boots, coat, dress, hat, jacket, jeans, pajamas, shirt, shoes, shorts, sneakers, socks, sweater, T-shirt, underwear

M

machine, magazine, magician, magnet, man, map, marbles, mask, match, mattress, meat, melon, mirror, money, mop, mouse, moustache, mushroom

36–39 **Magician,** behind/in front of, big/little, hot/cold, up/down, happy/sad, inside/outside, on/off, short/tall

NO

nail, neck, necklace, necktie, needle, nest, newspaper, night, nightgown, notebook, nut, oar, ocean, octopus, oil well, onion, orange, ostrich, owl

40–43 **Ocean,** ball, bathing suit, beach, bird, boat, comic book, fisherman, lighthouse, pail, sandwich, shark, shell, shovel, starfish, submarine, swimmer, towel, wave

PQ

pan, pants, parachute, park, parrot, pedal, piano, picture, pillow, pin, pineapple, pliers, pocket, puppet, purse, puzzle, queen

44–47 **Park,** break, buy, catch, climb, draw, drink, eat, fall, jump, kick, pull, push, read, run, sit, sleep, throw, walk

RS

rabbit, rainbow, record, ring, robot, rocket, rocking chair, rope, rug, saw, sewing machine, shoelace, smoke, snowman, spider, stamp, string, supermarket

48–51 **Supermarket,** bananas, beans, bread, butter, carrots, cereal, cheese, chicken, crackers, eggs, hamburger, hot dogs, juice, lettuce, milk, peanut butter, potatoes, rice

T

tail, teacher, teddy bear, telephone, throne, toaster, toes, toilet paper, tomato, tongue, tools, toothbrush, toothpaste, toys, tracks, train, triangle, trunk, turtle

52–55 **Teacher,** aquarium, board, book, bookcase, bulletin board, chalk, clock, crayons, desk, eraser, paint, paper, pencil, pencil sharpener, ruler, scissors, student, wastepaper basket

UVW

umbrella, vacuum cleaner, van, vase, vegetables, vest, violin, volcano, wagon, waiter, wall, watch, water, whale, wheelbarrow, wind, witch, woman

56–59 **Weather,** bush, cactus, cloud, fire, lightning, moon, mountain, rain, river, road, shadow, sky, sleeping bag, snake, snow, stars, sun, tent

XYZ

X-ray, xylophone, yarn, yo-yo, yolk, zebra, zipper, zoo

60–63 **Zoo,** bench, cage, camel, camera, eagle, elephant, giraffe, gorilla, hippopotamus, lion, monkey, panda, penguin, polar bear, rest rooms, seal, tiger, vet

1 one red rocket

2 two green grasshoppers

3 three black buttons

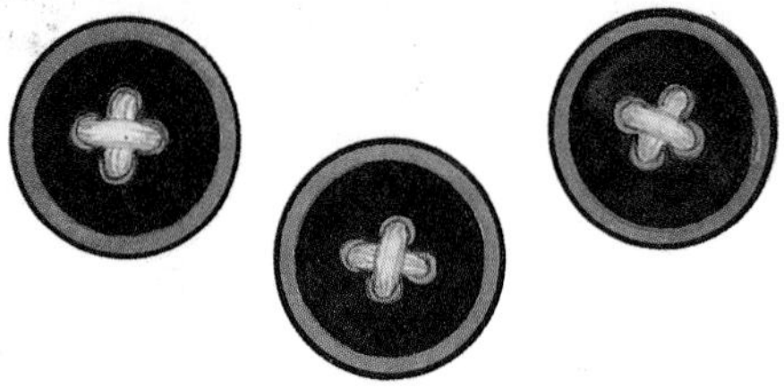

4 four yellow yo-yos

5 five brown bugs

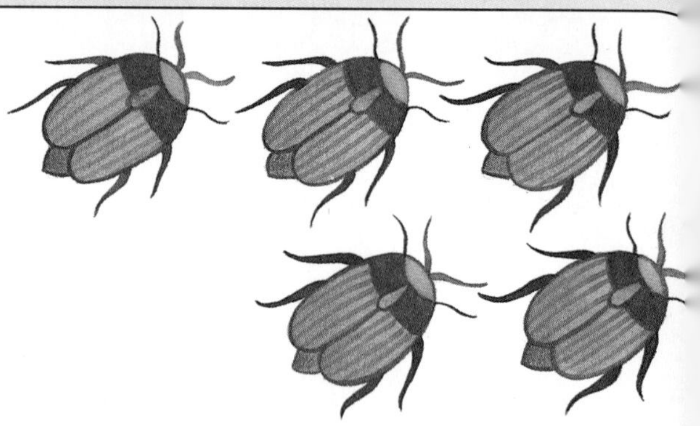

6 six white whales

7 seven orange owls

8 eight blue balls

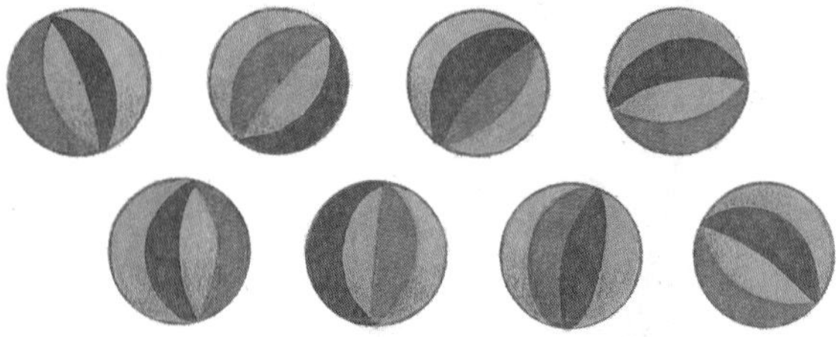

9 nine purple parrots

10 ten pink pigs

11
12
13
14
15

16
17
18
19
20

3

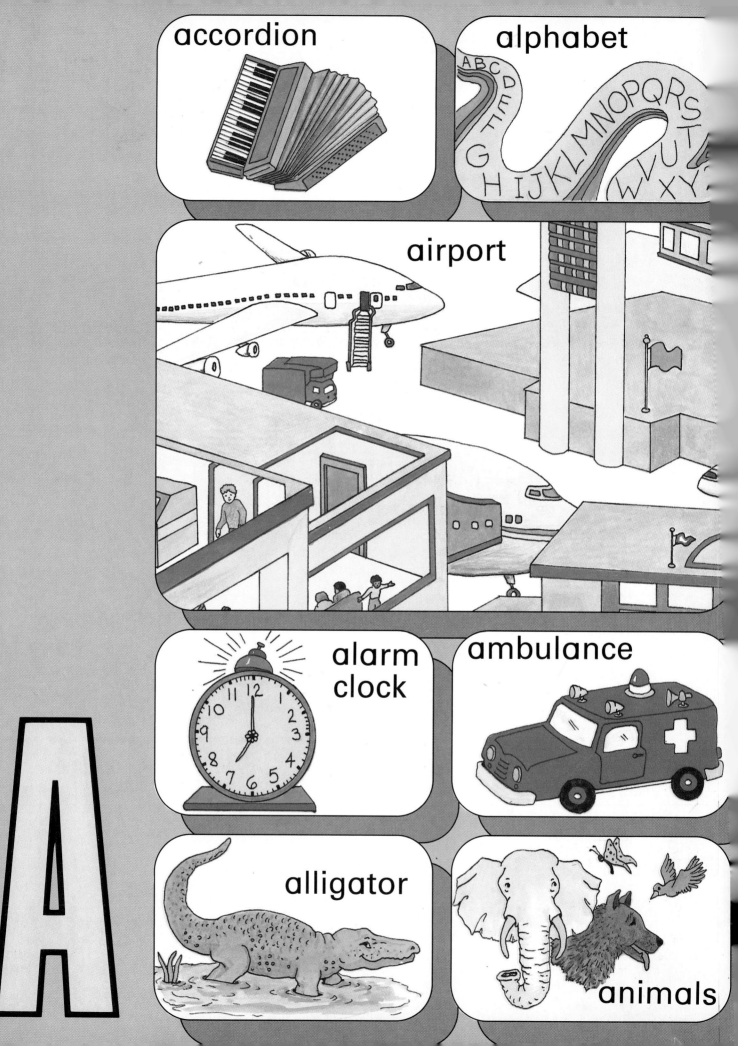

accordion

alphabet

airport

alarm clock

ambulance

A

alligator

animals

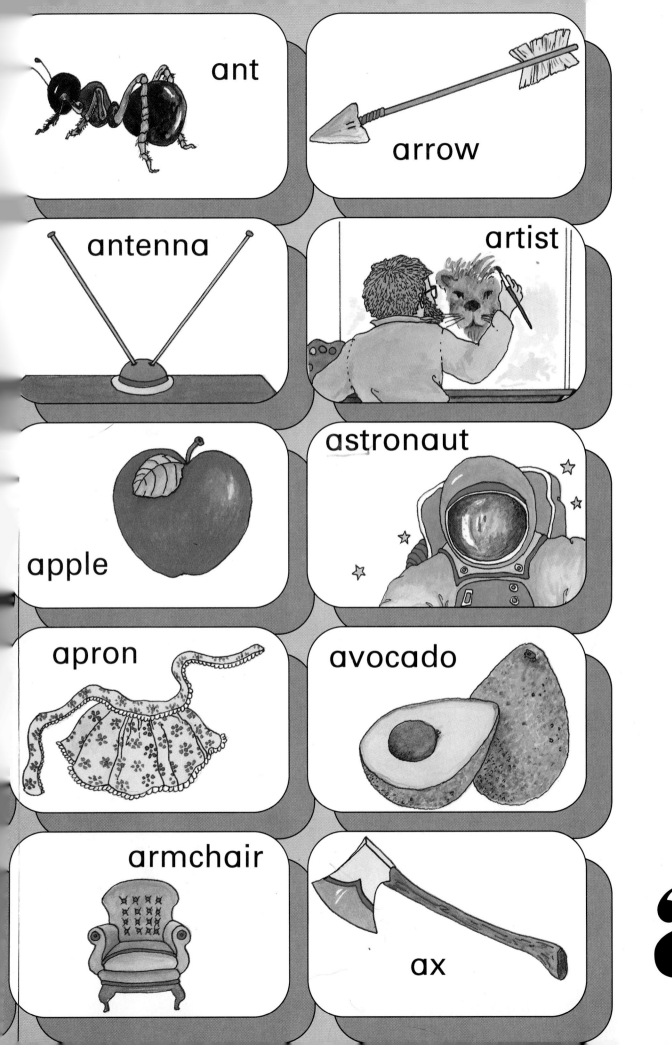

ant

arrow

antenna

artist

apple

astronaut

apron

avocado

armchair

ax

a

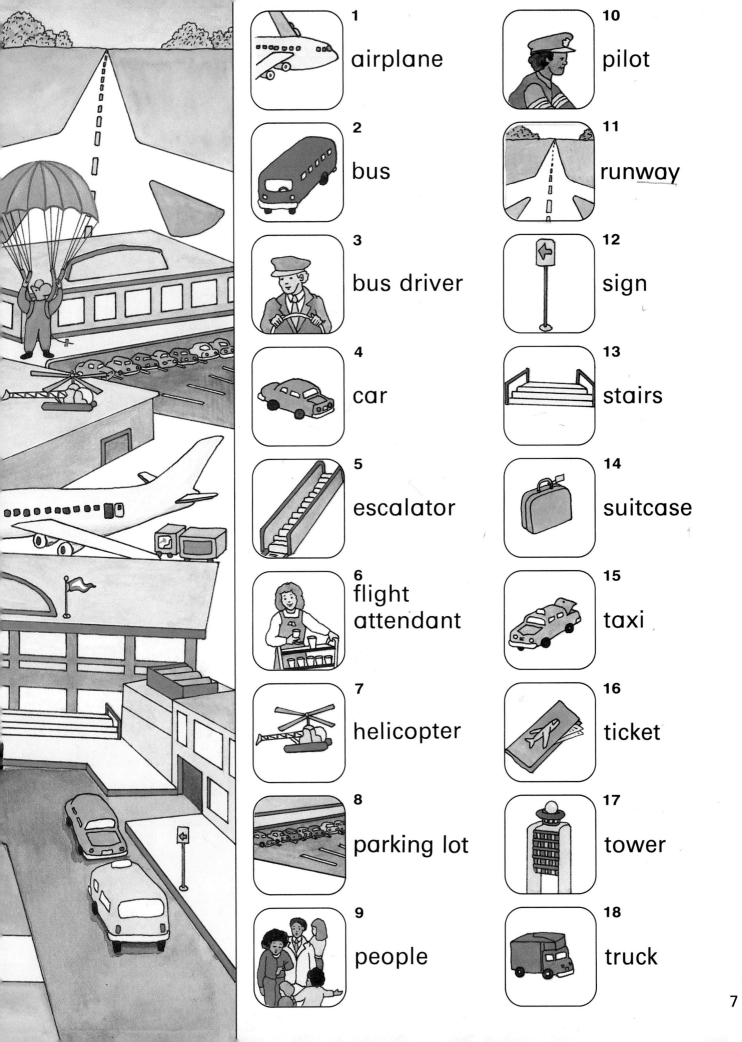

1 airplane

2 bus

3 bus driver

4 car

5 escalator

6 flight attendant

7 helicopter

8 parking lot

9 people

10 pilot

11 runway

12 sign

13 stairs

14 suitcase

15 taxi

16 ticket

17 tower

18 truck

B

bag

bee

balloon

bell

bat

beard

birthday party

bed

blanket

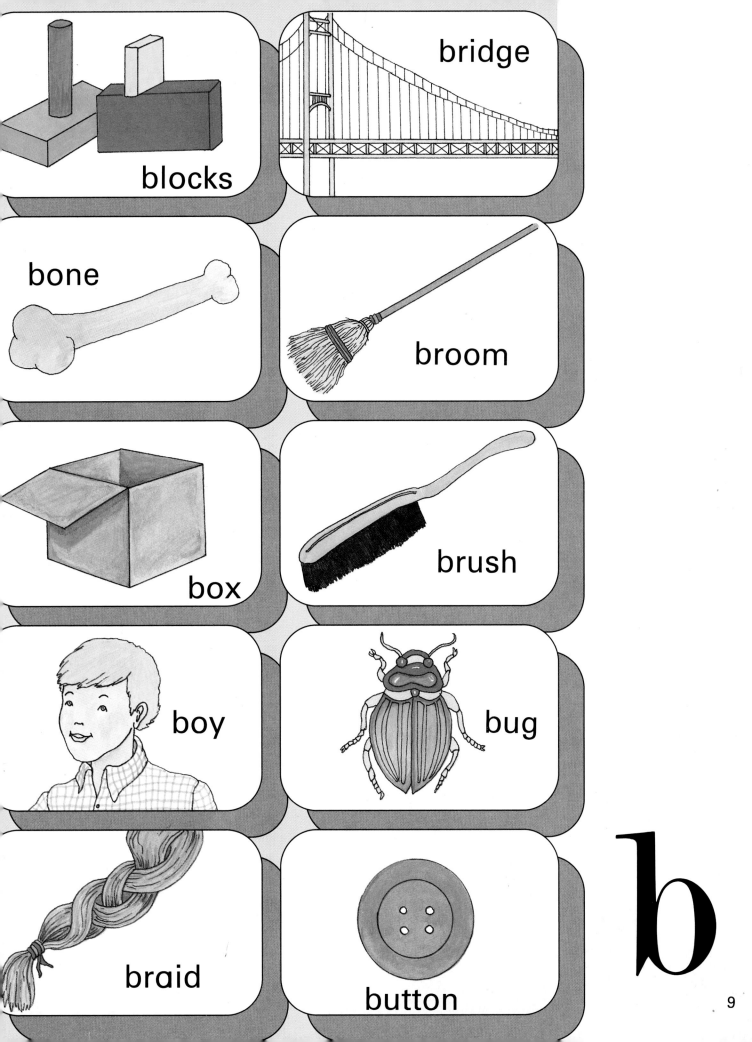

blocks

bridge

bone

broom

box

brush

boy

bug

braid

button

b

9

1 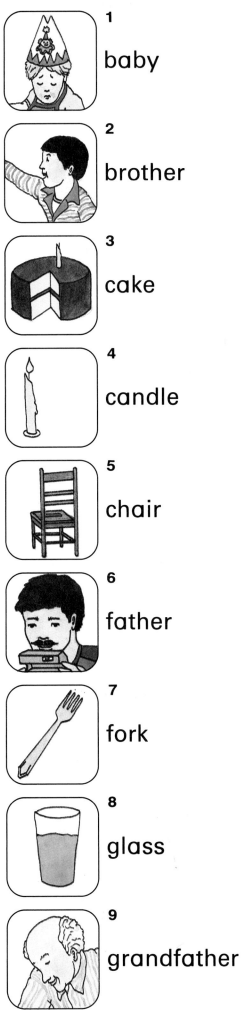 baby		**10** grandmother	

1 baby

2 brother

3 cake

4 candle

5 chair

6 father

7 fork

8 glass

9 grandfather

10 grandmother

11 knife

12 mother

13 napkin

14 plate

15 present

16 sister

17 spoon

18 table

cabbage

cannon

calendar

cat

calf

cherries

can

chimney

cane

chin

C

church

comb

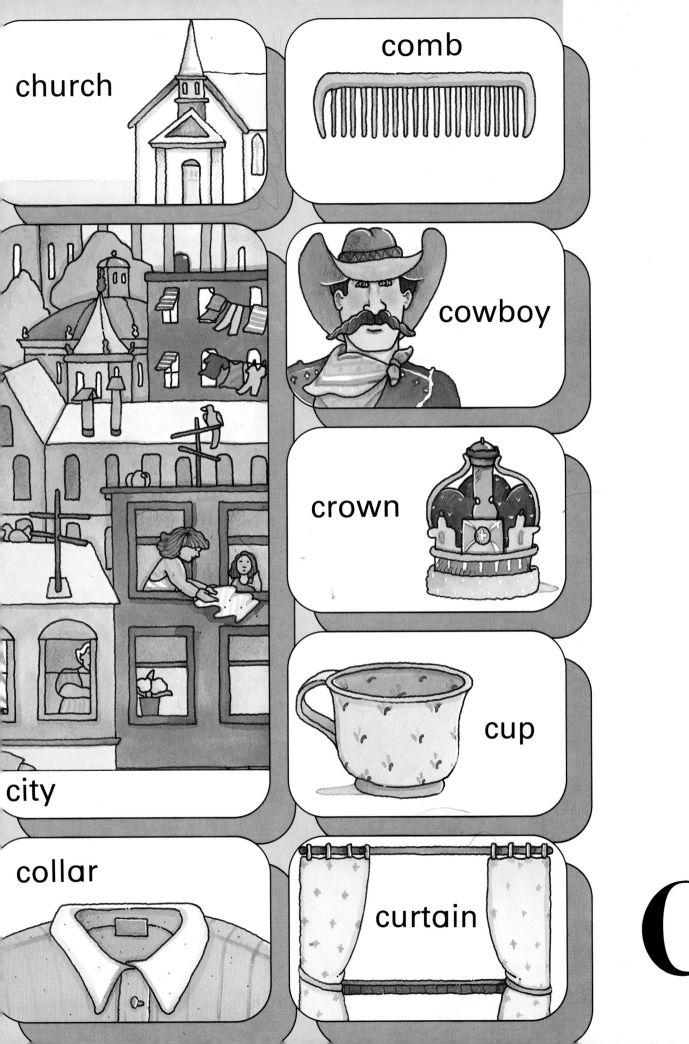

cowboy

crown

city

cup

collar

curtain

C

13

1 apartment house

2 bicycle

3 corner

4 fire escape

5 fire hydrant

6 garbage can

7 mailbox

8 motorcycle

9 office building

10 police officer

11 restaurant

12 roof

13 sidewalk

14 steps

15 store

16 street

17 streetlight

18 traffic light

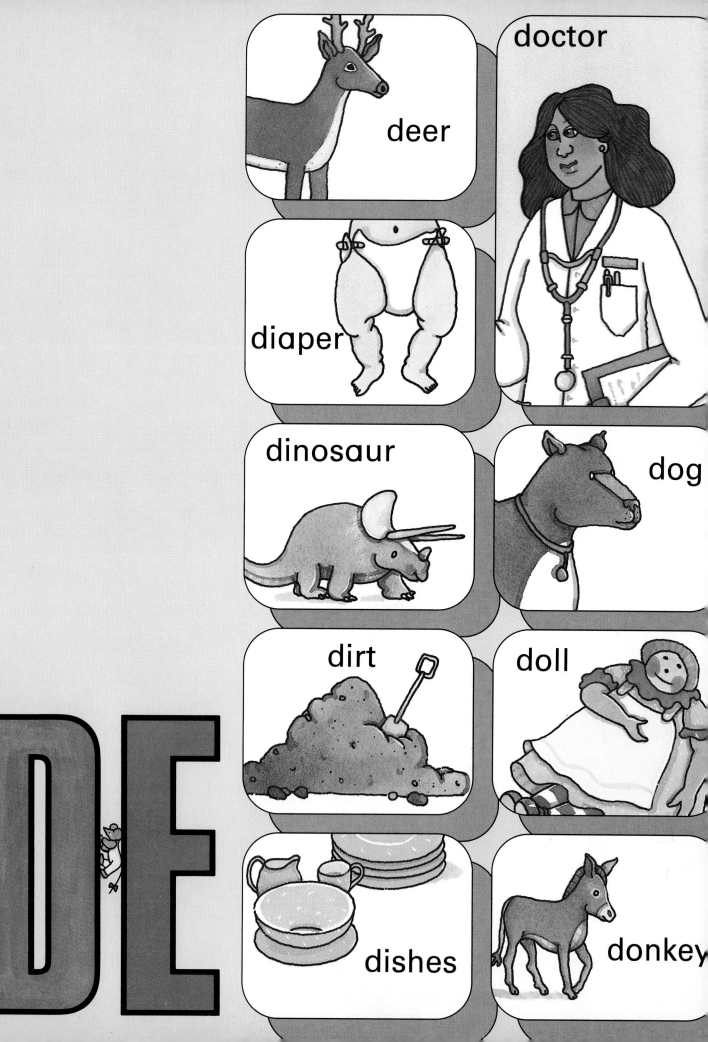

D E

deer

diaper

doctor

dinosaur

dog

dirt

doll

dishes

donkey

doughnut

earth

drawer

egg

drum

elbow

duck

elevator

earring

eraser

d e

17

1 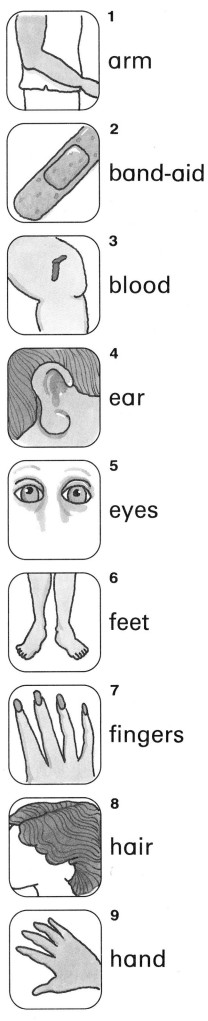 arm	**10** head
2 band-aid	**11** knee
3 blood	**12** leg
4 ear	**13** mouth
5 eyes	**14** nose
6 feet	**15** nurse
7 fingers	**16** stomach
8 hair	**17** teeth
9 hand	**18** thumb

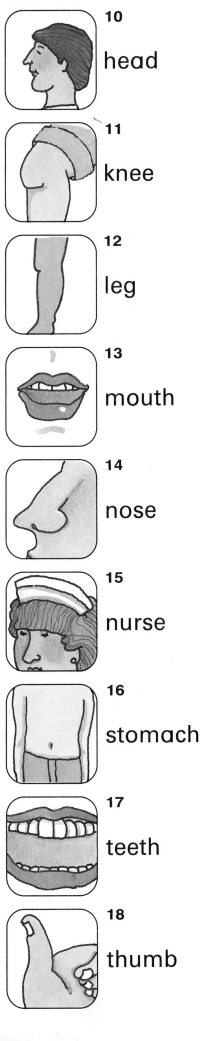

F

face

faucet

factory

feather

family

fish

fan

flashlight

farm

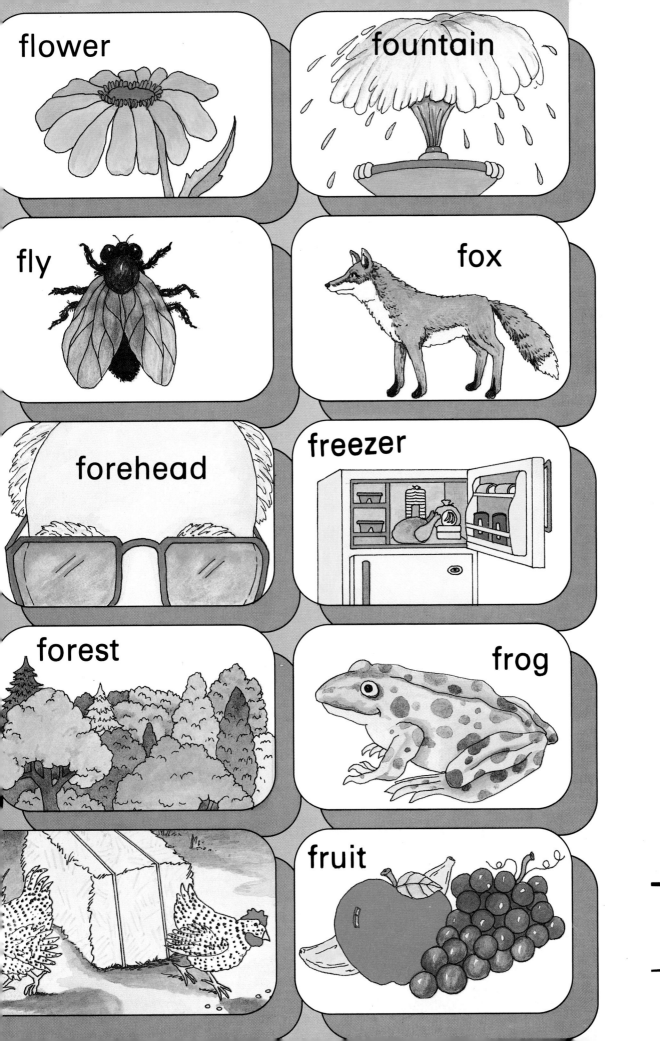

flower

fountain

fly

fox

forehead

freezer

forest

frog

fruit

f

1 barn 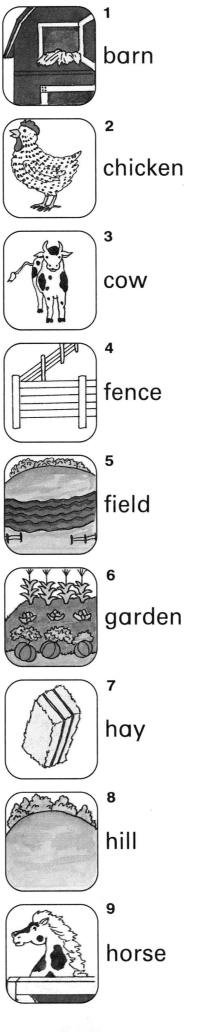	**10** mud
2 chicken	**11** pig
3 cow	**12** pond
4 fence	**13** porch
5 field	**14** rock
6 garden	**15** rooster
7 hay	**16** tire
8 hill	**17** tractor
9 horse	**18** tree

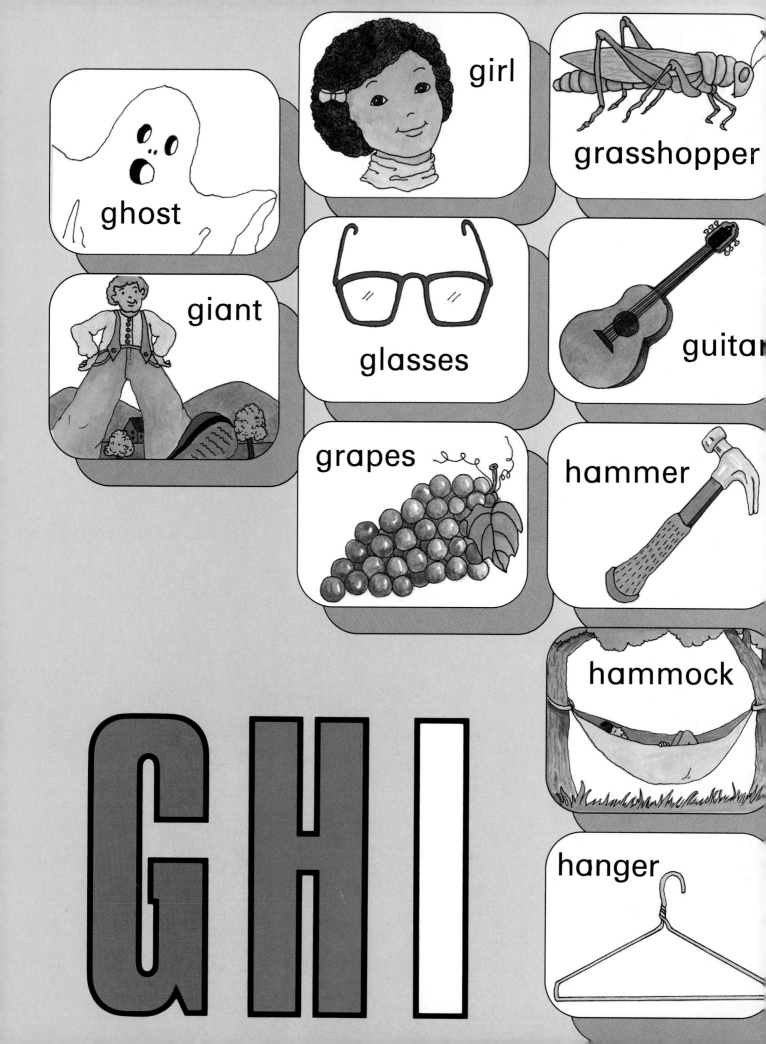

ghost

girl

grasshopper

giant

glasses

guitar

grapes

hammer

hammock

hanger

GHI

heart

ice

iron

hook

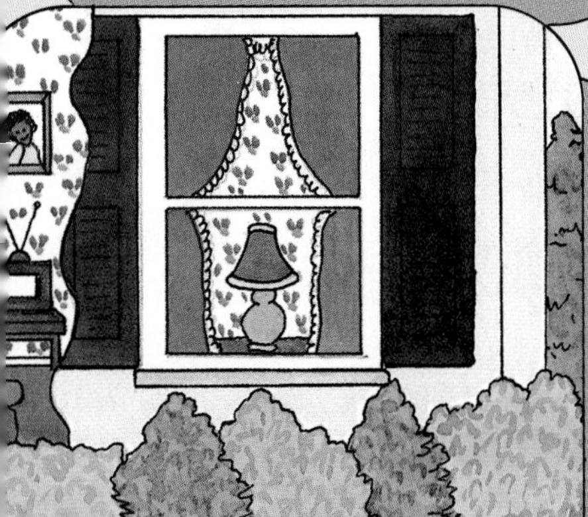

ice cream

island

horn

igloo

house

g h i

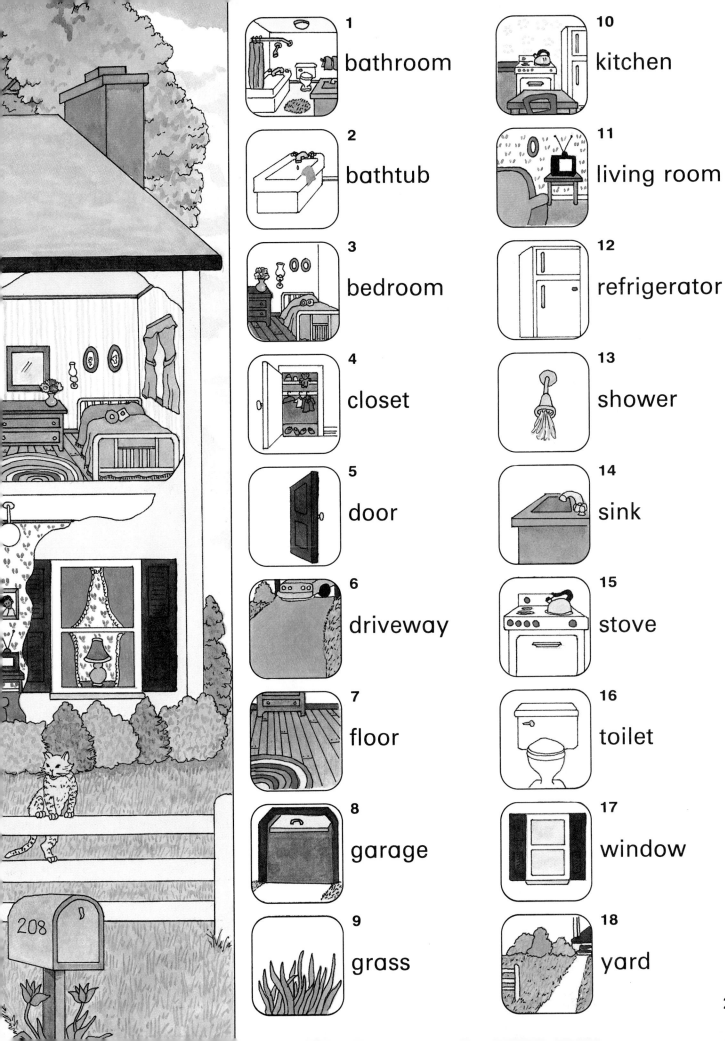

1 bathroom

2 bathtub

3 bedroom

4 closet

5 door

6 driveway

7 floor

8 garage

9 grass

10 kitchen

11 living room

12 refrigerator

13 shower

14 sink

15 stove

16 toilet

17 window

18 yard

208

27

J K

jail

jewel

jar

jeep

jelly

jobs

jellyfish

jump rope

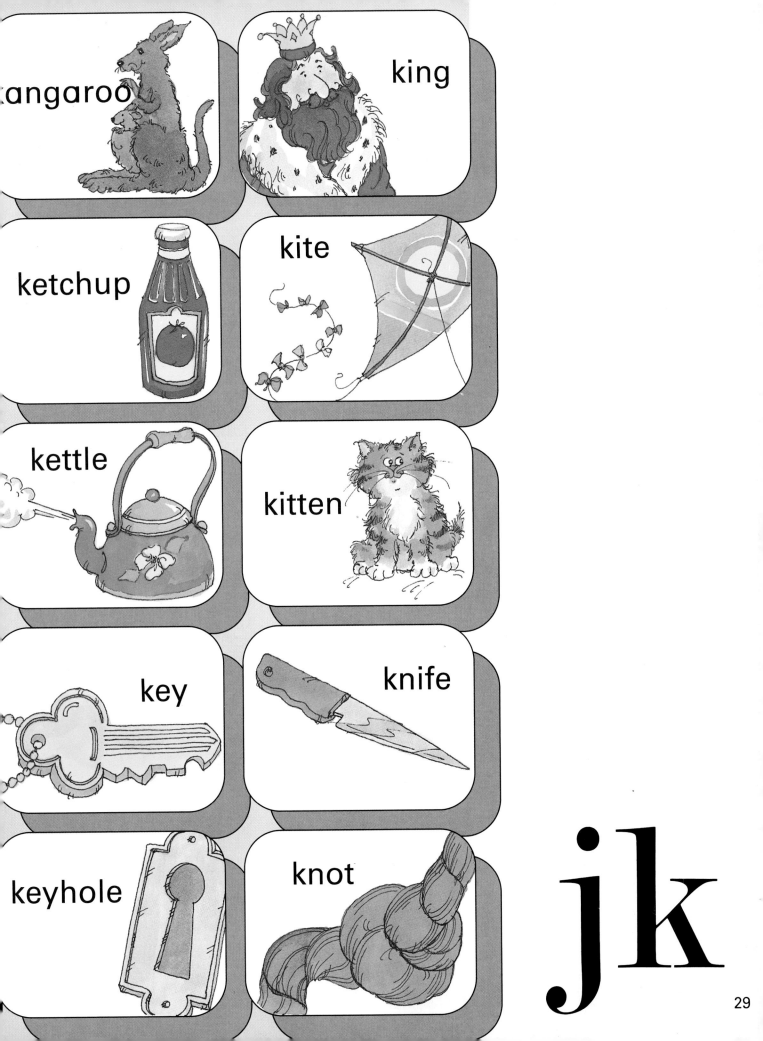

kangaroo

king

ketchup

kite

kettle

kitten

key

knife

keyhole

knot

jk

29

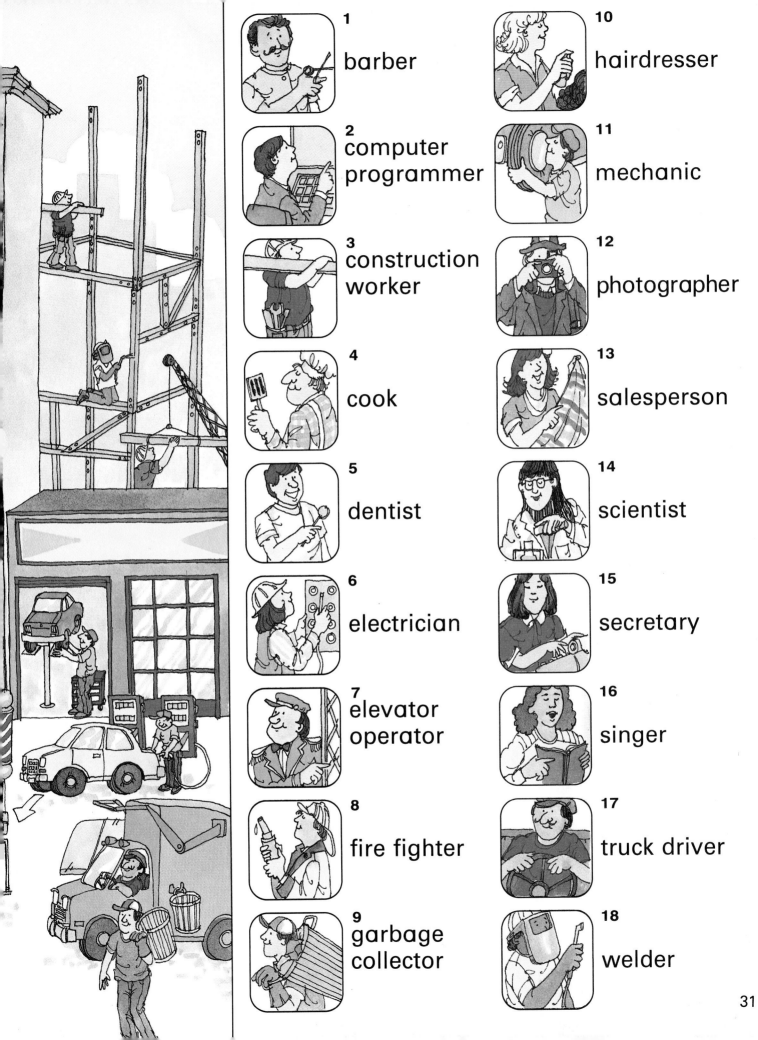

1 barber

2 computer programmer

3 construction worker

4 cook

5 dentist

6 electrician

7 elevator operator

8 fire fighter

9 garbage collector

10 hairdresser

11 mechanic

12 photographer

13 salesperson

14 scientist

15 secretary

16 singer

17 truck driver

18 welder

31

lace

lap

ladder

laundry

lake

leaf

lamb

lemon

lamp

letter

L

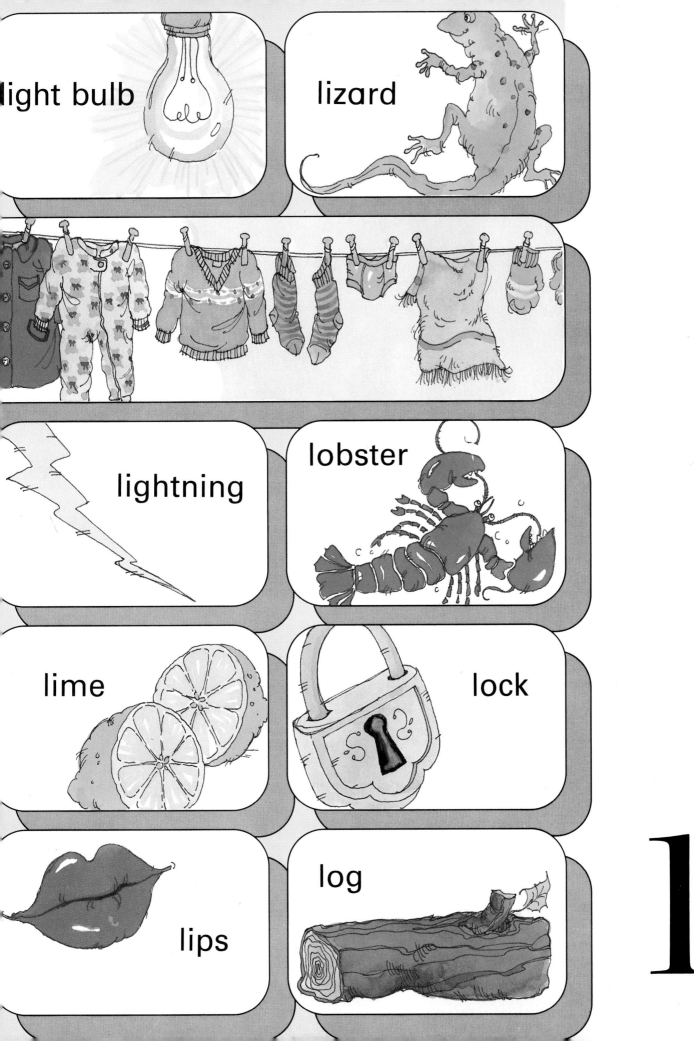

light bulb

lizard

lightning

lobster

lime

lock

lips

log

1

33

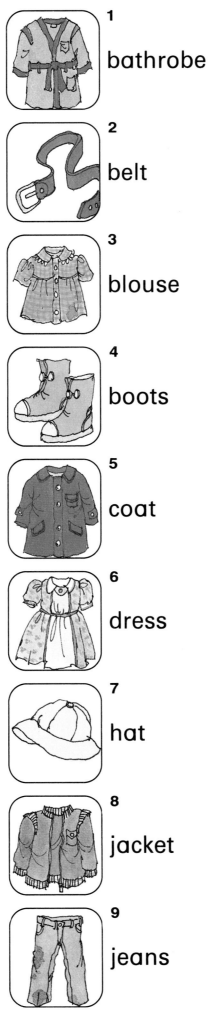

1 bathrobe

2 belt

3 blouse

4 boots

5 coat

6 dress

7 hat

8 jacket

9 jeans

10 pajamas

11 shirt

12 shoes

13 shorts

14 sneakers

15 socks

16 sweater

17 T-shirt

18 underwear

M

machine

magnet

magazine

man

map

magician

marbles

mask

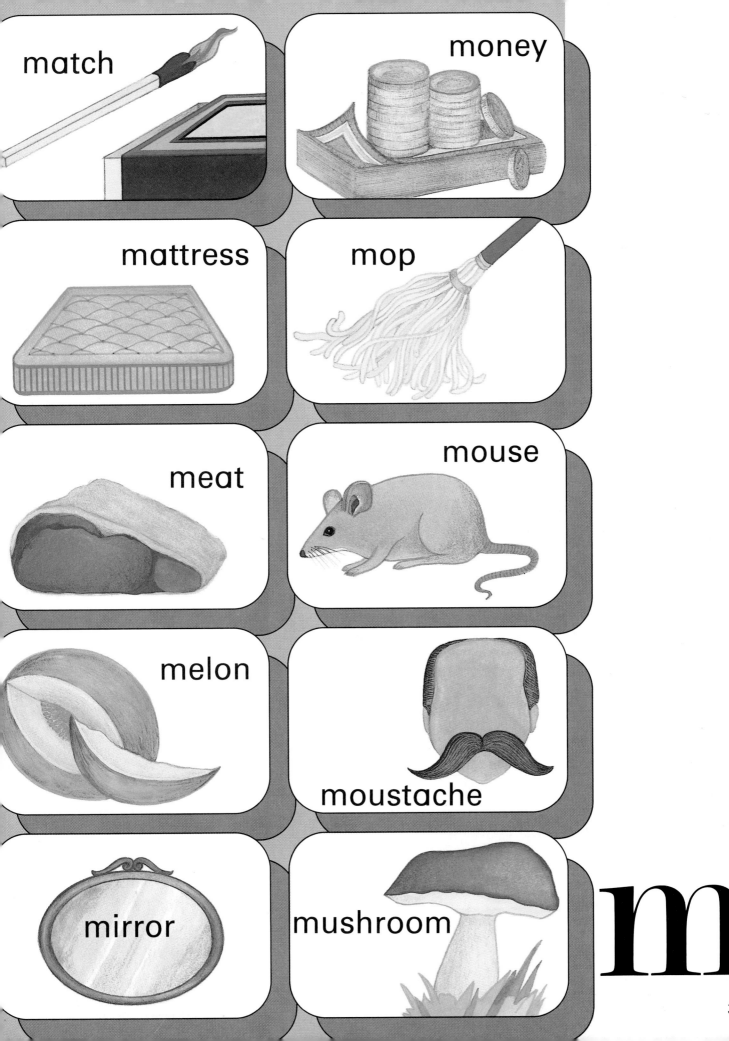

match

money

mattress

mop

meat

mouse

melon

moustache

mirror

mushroom

m

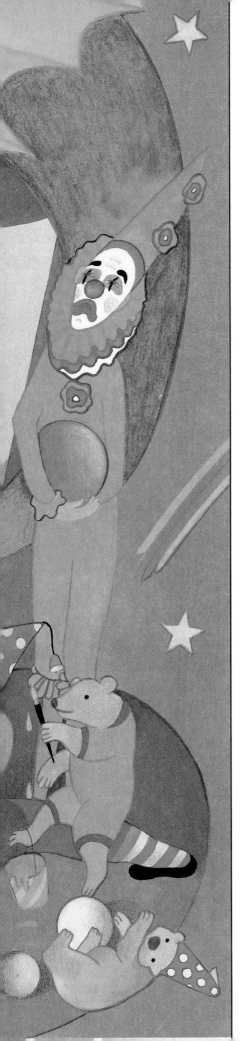

1 in front of	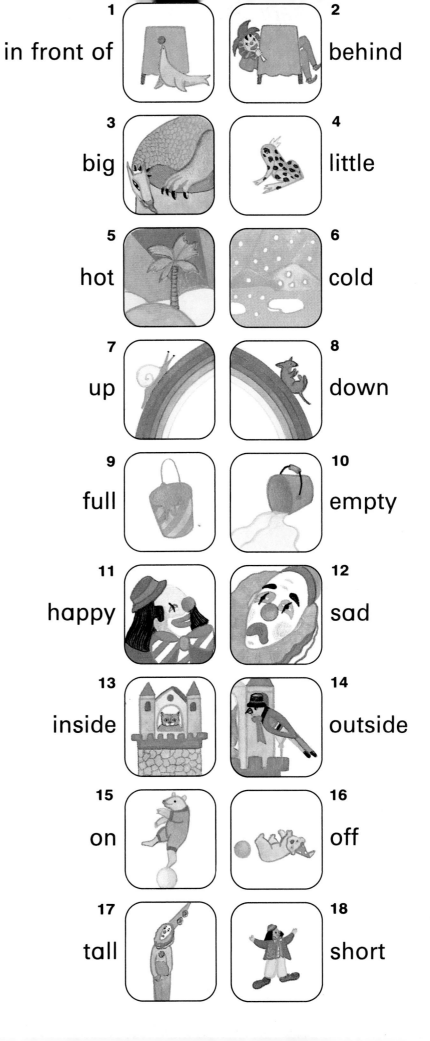	2 behind
3 big		4 little
5 hot		6 cold
7 up		8 down
9 full		10 empty
11 happy		12 sad
13 inside		14 outside
15 on		16 off
17 tall		18 short

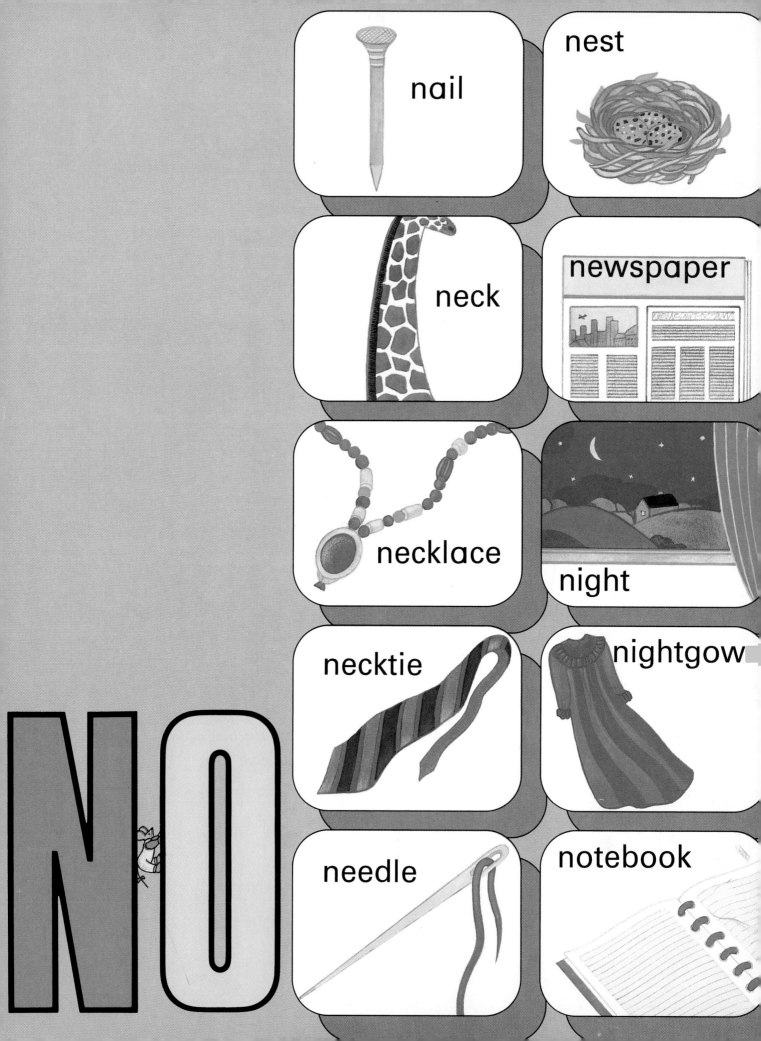

nail

nest

neck

newspaper

necklace

night

necktie

nightgown

needle

notebook

N O

nut

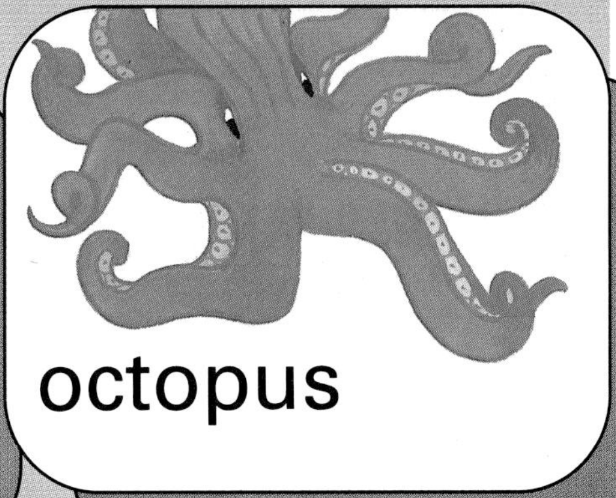

octopus

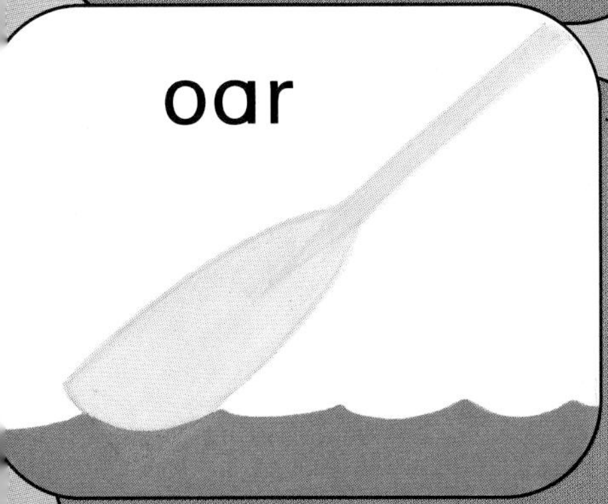

oar

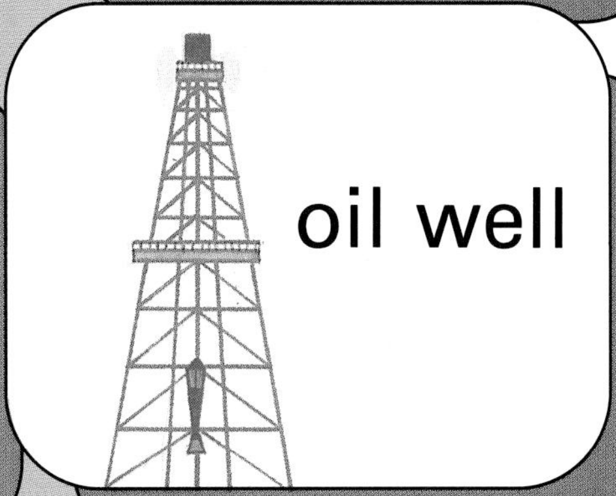

oil well

onion

orange

ostrich

ocean

n·o

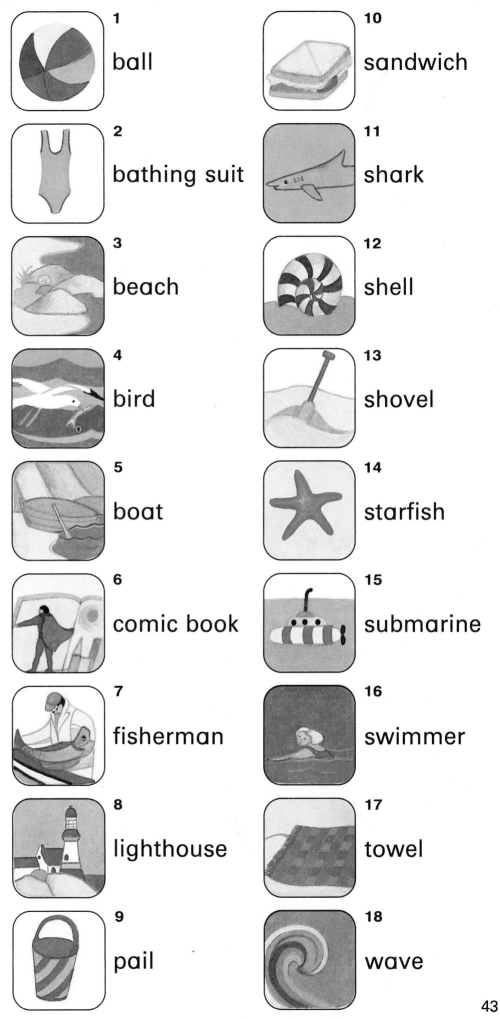

1 ball

2 bathing suit

3 beach

4 bird

5 boat

6 comic book

7 fisherman

8 lighthouse

9 pail

10 sandwich

11 shark

12 shell

13 shovel

14 starfish

15 submarine

16 swimmer

17 towel

18 wave

pan

parrot

pants

pedal

parachute

piano

park

PQ

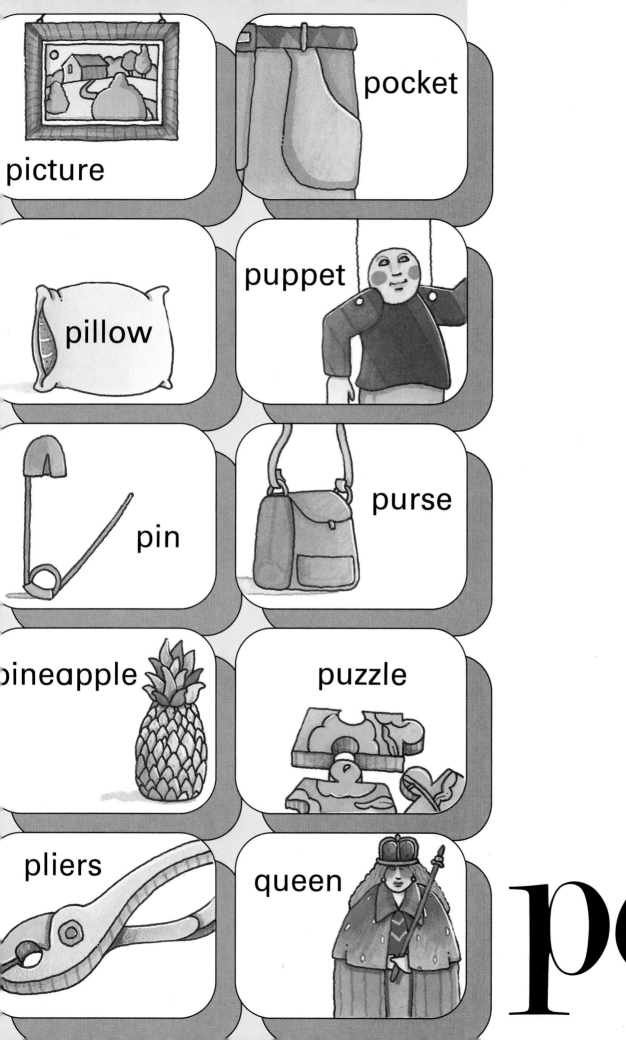

picture

pocket

pillow

puppet

pin

purse

pineapple

puzzle

pliers

queen

pq

45

1	break	**10**	kick
2	buy	**11**	pull
3	catch	**12**	push
4	climb	**13**	read
5	draw	**14**	run
6	drink	**15**	sit
7	eat	**16**	sleep
8	fall	**17**	throw
9	jump	**18**	walk

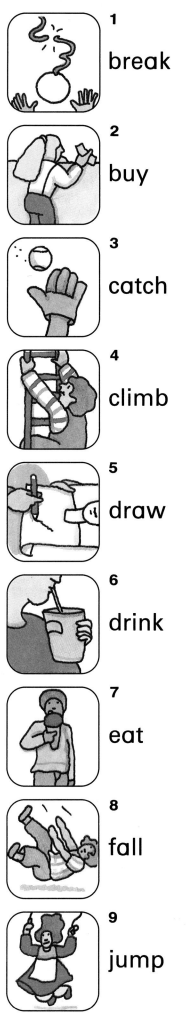

47

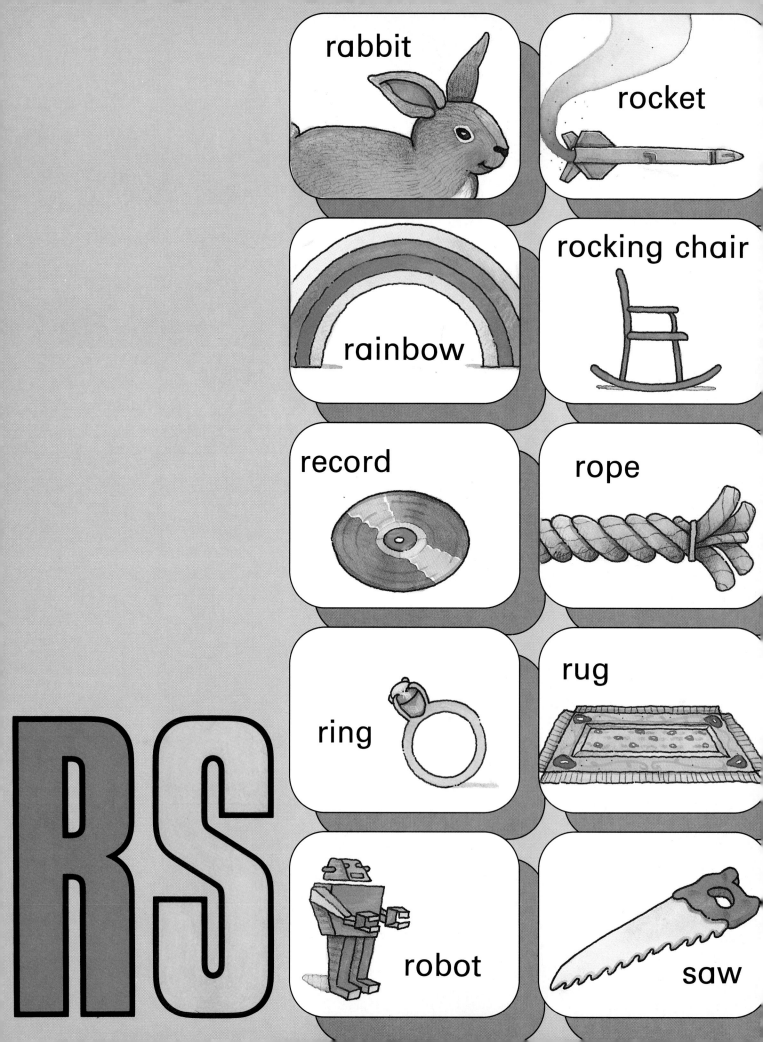

rabbit

rocket

rainbow

rocking chair

record

rope

ring

rug

robot

saw

R S

sewing machine

stamp

shoelace

string

smoke

snowman

spider

supermarket

rs

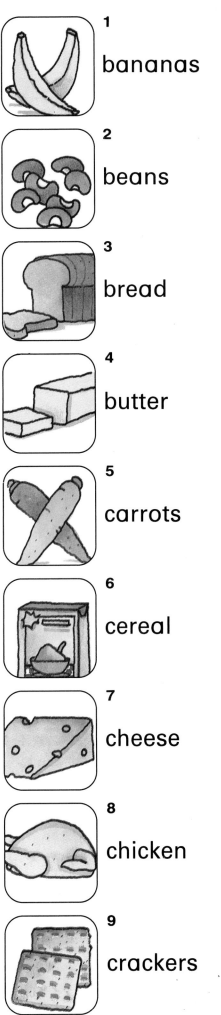

1	bananas	**10**	eggs
2	beans	**11**	hamburger
3	bread	**12**	hot dogs
4	butter	**13**	juice
5	carrots	**14**	lettuce
6	cereal	**15**	milk
7	cheese	**16**	peanut butter
8	chicken	**17**	potatoes
9	crackers	**18**	rice

tail

throne

teacher

toaster

toes

teddy bear

toilet paper

telephone

tomato

T

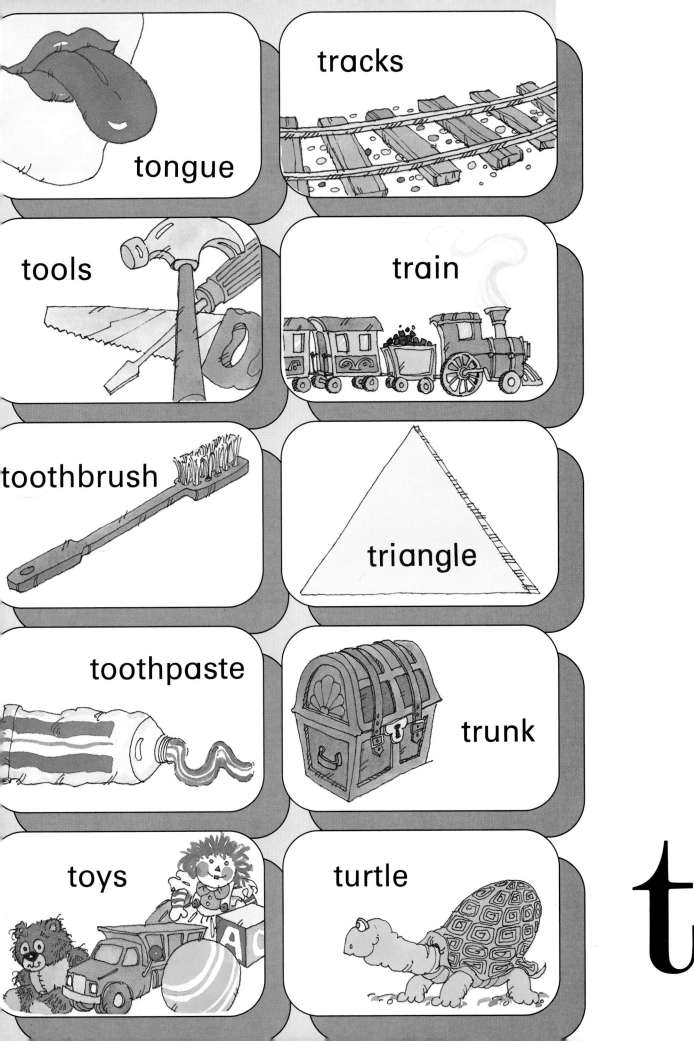

tongue

tracks

tools

train

toothbrush

triangle

toothpaste

trunk

toys

turtle

t

1	aquarium	10	eraser
2	board	11	paint
3	book	12	paper
4	bookcase	13	pencil
5	bulletin board	14	pencil sharpener
6	chalk	15	ruler
7	clock	16	scissors
8	crayons	17	student
9	desk	18	wastepaper basket

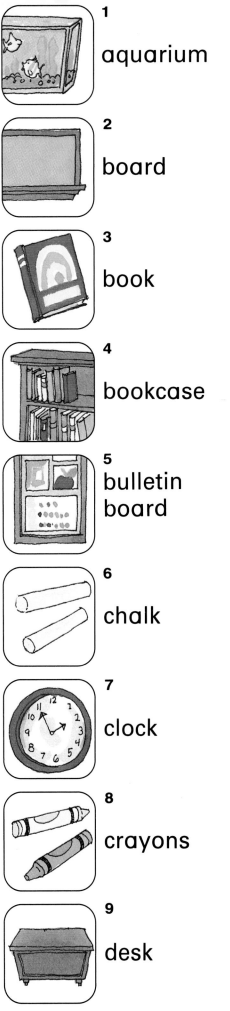
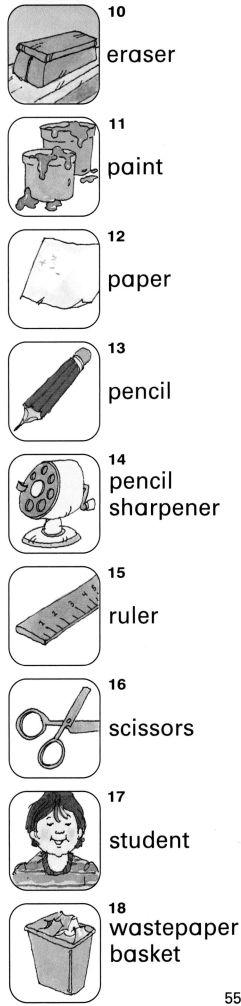

55

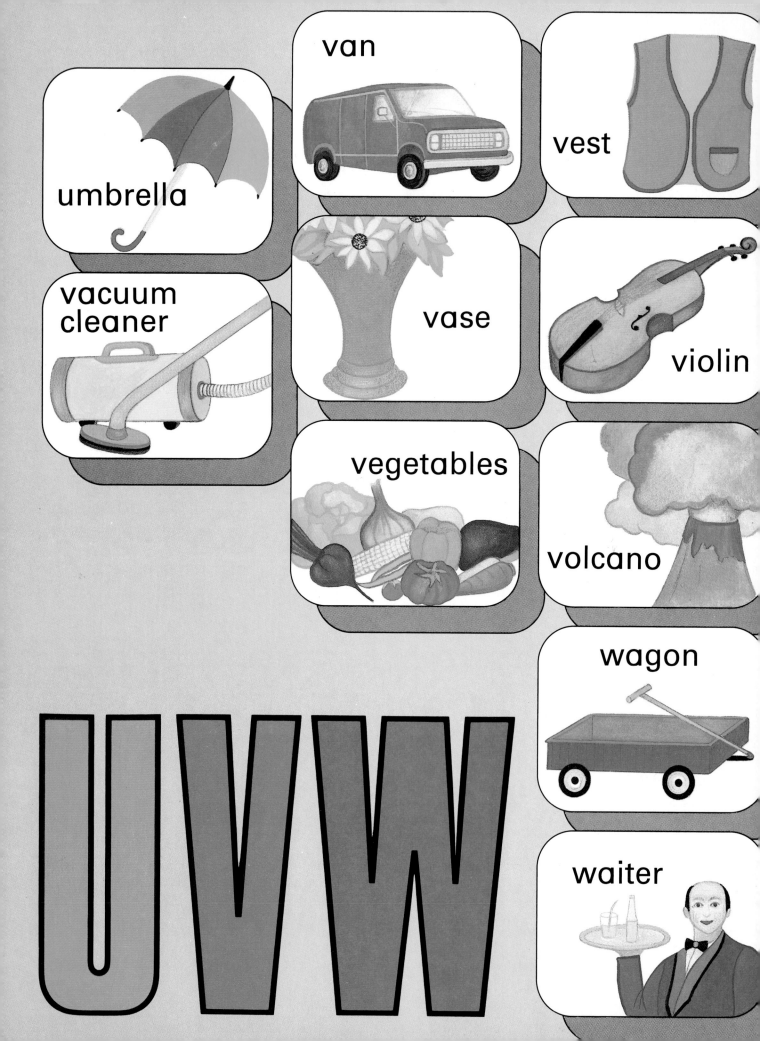

umbrella

vacuum cleaner

van

vase

vegetables

vest

violin

volcano

wagon

waiter

U V W

wall

watch

water

whale

wheelbarrow

wind

witch

woman

u v w

1 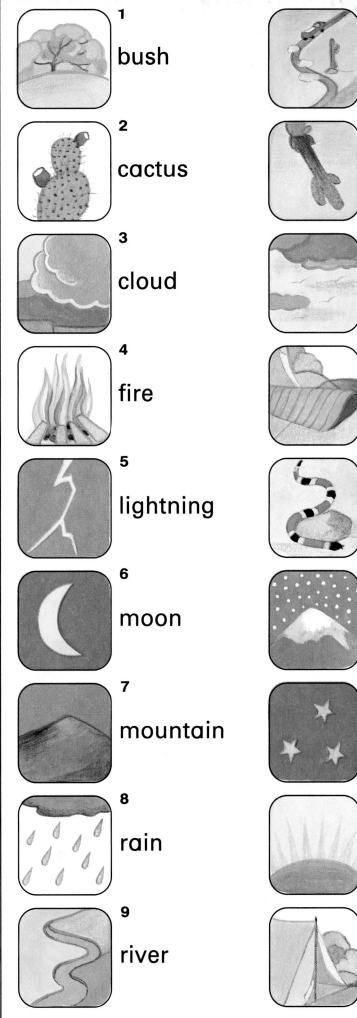 bush	**10** road
2 cactus	**11** shadow
3 cloud	**12** sky
4 fire	**13** sleeping bag
5 lightning	**14** snake
6 moon	**15** snow
7 mountain	**16** stars
8 rain	**17** sun
9 river	**18** tent

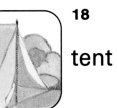

59

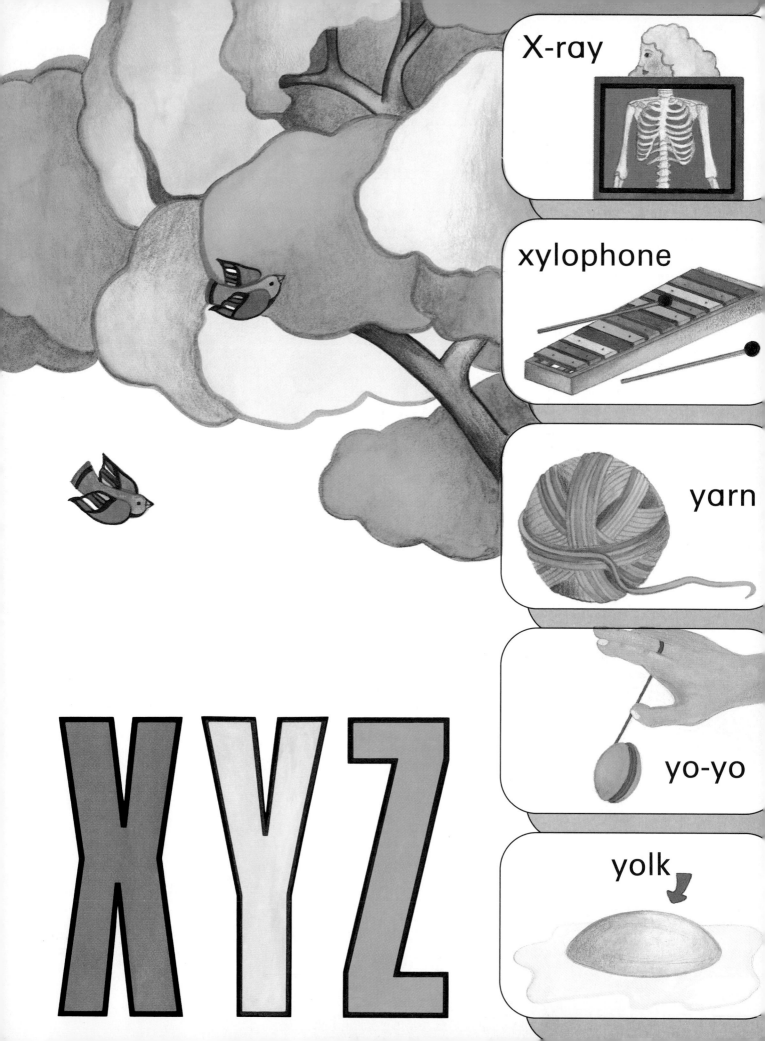

X-ray

xylophone

yarn

yo-yo

yolk

XYZ

zebra

zipper

zoo

xyz

1 bench	**10** lion
2 cage	**11** monkey
3 camel	**12** panda
4 camera	**13** penguin
5 eagle	**14** polar bear
6 elephant	**15** rest rooms
7 giraffe	**16** seal
8 gorilla	**17** tiger
9 hippopotamus	**18** vet

USING THE DICTIONARY IN THE CLASSROOM

The following ideas and activities should help you develop your own ways of using this book. We encourage you to experiment with a wide range of expansion activities. A page may be used several times, in different ways on different days, and children will enjoy the "return trip." Use your own discretion as to how early and how far you can take these ideas with your students.

Numbers and Colors Pages

For beginning level students, these pages will provide key vocabulary needed for discussing the pictures on the following pages. With beginning students, you will want to supplement these pages with lots of different number and color activities. Sing counting and color songs. Encourage students to count objects and people around them (pencils, books, windows, children wearing white socks, etc.). Play active counting games while bouncing balls or skipping rope. Hand number cards to the children and have them line themselves up in order. Have children stand up or sit down when you call their number. Ask children to group themselves according to those wearing blue or green. On command, have each student find and touch something red or yellow. If students are not familiar with the English alphabet, take this opportunity to teach it by singing the ABC song, and pointing to the letters listed in the Table of Contents.

Letter Pages

1 Present the words on the page in sequence first. Let students repeat them after you. If some of your students are already familiar with some of the words, let *them* present those words. Remember to allow the students plenty of time to study the pictures.

2 After the words have been introduced and practiced, name the pictures out of sequence. Have students point to the correct pictures.

3 If students are ready, work on the concept of alphabetizing by second or third letters.

4 Students with names beginning with the focus letter(s) should write their names (or see them written) on the board. (If students are ready, they can put their names in alphabetical order.) You may want to give these students a special "star" role in the lesson. For example, they can assume the role of teacher and ask their classmates, *Is this a button? What's this?* Or they can name pictures on the page at random while the other students point.

5 Use a graded question chain to practice the new vocabulary. You can adapt these questions to the skill level of your group.
Yes-No questions: (point) *Is this an apple?*
Alternative questions: *Is this an apron or an astronaut?*
Information questions: *What's this? What's below the apron? What's next to the alligator? What's after the apple?*

6 As soon as students are ready, ask classification questions about the vocabulary words. Often several words will fit a category. For example, on the "A" page, you might ask:
What is red? (the apple, the ambulance)
What is sharp? (the arrow, the ax)
What makes a noise? (the accordion, the alarm clock, the ambulance, etc.)

7 Draw attention to the initial letter in each target word and the initial sound represented by this letter. To practice auditory discrimination, say a list of words and ask students to repeat each word that begins with the target letter sound. Have them clap their hands (or stand up) when they hear a word that *does not* begin with that sound. Example: *boy, big, Bobby, car, boots, bus, girl . . .*

8 On some pages, one letter represents several sounds. For example, on the "C" page, children are introduced to the sounds /k/ as in *cat,* and /ch/ as in *chin.* Help your students group the words beginning with the /ch/ sound, and note the initial digraph *ch* in each of these words. On the "G" page, both the hard and soft *g* sounds are illustrated. If possible, elicit other *g* as /j/ words from your students. *I'm thinking of a word that begins with the /j/ sound. It's a room in the school where you can run, and jump rope, and play ball. (gym)*

9 Always encourage the children to name other words they know that begin with the target letter(s). (Students need not limit themselves to nouns). As each letter page after "A" is covered, go back to previous scenes and ask the students if they see other words beginning with the same letter. For example, looking for "C" words in the Birthday Party scene, students will find the labeled words *cake, candle,* and *chair.* Searching the scene, they may also be able to identify *camera, clock, coffee, cup, cupboard, canisters, counter, children, chocolate icing,* etc.

10 You may wish to establish a weekly "My Dictionary" project. Each child can choose new words discovered during lessons, illustrate, and label them. (If your group is not ready to write the words, you can print them yourself and have the children trace them, or just skip that stage for now.) Each child should work orally with his or her own dictionary, however—presenting new pages to classmates, asking and answering questions about the pictured words, and using the words in simple sentences whenever possible.

The Scenes

The scenes are multi-purpose language motivators. Each can be used for several lessons emphasizing different skills. The scenes help students build their vocabulary, learn to use the new words in meaningful sentences, practice verb tenses and other grammatical structures, and develop comprehension skills. The following steps can be used to introduce these pages.

1 Remember to let the children find the mouse in each scene. Encourage the students to say whatever they can about what the mouse is doing, what it is wearing, how it is feeling, where it was in the previous scene, etc.

2 Teach the eighteen labeled words next, or if you prefer, have students study the scene first. Ask, *What is this picture about?* (main idea). Have students name any objects in the scene they know. If you wish, write this student-generated word list on the board.

3 After teaching the labeled words, have students locate each word in the large picture scene. Ask students to use the words in simple sentences. Encourage students to add words that fit the theme (or semantic field) of each scene. For example, they may know other action verbs for the Park, more antonyms for the Magician, etc. If you wish, write these words on cards and let the students illustrate them. You can display these new vocabulary words in alphabetical order on the classroom wall.

Also, don't neglect the opportunity to let students question you about a pictured word which they may be able to name in their native language, but not in English. It should prove to be true that individuals will constantly point and ask, *What's this?*, or *How do you say this in English?*

Discussion and Story Building

1 The scenes lend themselves beautifully to story building. At an elementary level, this can take the form of list building, in an activity modeled on the game "I Packed My Grandmother's Trunk." For example, using the Supermarket scene, one child can begin, *In the store I see cheese.* The next player will add, *In the store I see cheese and (a box of) cereal.* The third player might say, *In the store I see cheese, cereal, and eggs.* At more advanced levels, each child can offer a sentence (or phrase) about something in the picture scene. Write the sentences down, creating a group story, then have the class read their story aloud.

Some scenes—the Laundry, the Doctor's Office, the Farm, the Ocean, and the Birthday Party—lend themselves to sequential stories. Encourage students to name the characters and tell or write a story.

2 In discussing the scenes, you will want to ask questions that make the students search for details, draw conclusions, and predict outcomes. The following and parallel questions could be asked about the Birthday Party. Accept single word answers, especially if your questions use tenses the students have yet to master.

Whose birthday is it? How do you know? How old is the little boy? How do you know? How old is his brother/mother/grandfather, etc.?

Did the family buy the cake or make it at home? How do you know?

Is the little boy happy or sad? Why?

What are his brother and sister doing? What do you think will happen next?

How will the sister feel then? What do you think she will do?

3 Encourage students to relate the scenes to themselves, their families, and their experiences. The following and parallel questions could be asked about the Laundry scene.

What color is the sweater in the picture? Who is wearing a green sweater today? Who is wearing a sweater that is not green? What color is your sweater? What's your favorite color? Does the sweater in the picture have buttons? How is (Ann's) sweater different from the sweater in the picture? How is it the same? Who is doing the laundry in the picture? Who does the laundry at your house? Does s(he) do it at home, or at another place? Do you help with the laundry? Do you do other jobs at home?

4 Whenever possible, encourage students to incorporate their outside knowledge (and mainstream curriculum concepts) into the discussion. The following questions might be asked about the cow in the Farm scene:

What is a baby cow called? What does a cow eat? Where does a cow live? How does a farmer take care of a cow? What food do we get from a cow? Do you like milk? Is milk good for you? Why? What foods are made from milk?

Vocabulary Development and Expansion

Teach songs, play games, and plan activities that build on the vocabulary areas presented in each scene. Here are a few suggestions:

The City
Show the children how to play "Twenty Questions" in pairs or in a group. One child chooses an object or person in the City scene. The other(s) must guess that object or person by asking yes/no questions: *Is it a person? Does it have wheels?* etc.

The Doctor
Teach singing games such as "Head, Shoulders, Knees, and Toes", "Looby Loo", and "Hokey, Pokey".

The Farm
Pin the name of an animal on each student's back. Students must guess their animal name by asking their classmates yes/no questions: *Do I have four legs? Can I fly? Am I bigger than a goat?* You can also teach the song, "Old McDonald Had a Farm."

The House

Ask students to draw their own homes, and show family members in the scene.

Jobs
Have volunteers pantomime jobs. Their classmates must guess the name of the occupation.

The Laundry
Have each child illustrate one of the 18 items. When you name a category, children with appropriate words can jump up, holding the correct picture word over their heads. Sample categories:

Something you wear on your feet (head, legs, etc.)

Something that has the letter L in it.
Something that begins with the letter S.
Something that can have buttons.
Something that rhymes with *car.*
Parallel work can be devised for every scene.

The Park
Make flashcards for the 18 action words. In silence, show the words to the class. The children must mime the actions shown. (Run, Jump, Sit, Walk, Climb, Sleep.) Teach the song, "If You're Happy and You Know It," using verb phrases from the Picture Scene (*kick a ball, climb a ladder*, etc.).

In sum, the language experiences that can be developed from this dictionary are virtually endless, since *several thousand* words are actually pictured. Don't be afraid to experiment—there is no one "best way" to use this book. Above all, enjoy the adventure in language learning with your children.

Word List